A Celebration of
BRITISH COLUMBIA FOODS
Souvenir Cookbook

Ministry of Agriculture, Fisheries and Food

Celebrating 100 Years of Achievement

Concept, Design,
Photography and
Photo Selection
Karl Spreitz

Art and Design
Assistance, Typesetting
Laurel Miller

Copy Editor
Linda Eversole

Editorial Assistance
Karen Speirs

B.C. Food Consultant
Mona Brun

First Nations
Contributions
Mary Gouchie
Beverly Antoine

Heart & Stroke Foundation
of B.C. & Yukon
Deb Jones

**British Columbia Ministry of Agriculture,
Fisheries and Food Centennial Committee**
Supervising Co-ordinator
Brooke C. Tomlin

Beautiful British Columbia
A Division of Great Pacific Industries Inc.
President
John L. Thomson

Director Publishing & Manufacturing
Tony Owen

Colour Separations and Film
WYSIWYG Graphics Inc.

Printing
Ronalds Printing, Vancouver, BC

Canadian Cataloguing in Publication Data
Main entry under title:
Celebration of British Columbia Food

Includes index.
ISBN 0-920431-00-3 (bound)
ISBN 0-920431-01-1 (pbk.)

1. Cookery, Canadian – British Columbia style. 2. Cookery –
British Columbia. I. Beautiful British Columbia Magazine
(Firm)

TX715.6.C44 1994   641.49711   C94-910626-7

All Photos by Karl Spreitz except:
page 9 Ted Galvin; page 16 Harry Tungate;
page 35 Doreen Collinge; page 38 Peter Thompson;
page 39 Betty Brownlee; page 60 Stacey Fehr;
page 62 Julie C. Bohnet; page 65 Kan Chew;
page 67 Lawrence Loiseau; page 72 Mark Wessner;
page 73 Karin L. Jungh; page 77 Rob Smith;
page 78 Bill Amos; page 78 Cec Johnson;
page 79 N. Jeffrey.

Table of Contents

Premier's Message

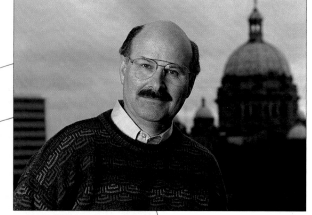

Premier Mike Harcourt

August 1994

Dear Friends:

On behalf of the people of British Columbia, it's my pleasure to welcome everyone to our beautiful province.

In the best tradition of the Commonwealth Games, British Columbians have pulled together to ensure the athletic competitions, cultural gatherings and festivals will prove a memorable celebration for you. What you see around you and throughout Greater Victoria is testimony to their hard work and spirit of cooperation.

We're also building on the Games' traditions with a number of innovations. Aboriginal people, on whose traditional territory the Games are being held, have been actively involved in preparations. Athletes with a disability are participating for the first time in Commonwealth Games' history. And a record number of events are highlighting women athletes.

With these developments, and with the commitment and dedication of British Columbians, I'm confident the XV Commonwealth Games will truly fulfill their motto as the "friendly games" for one and all.

May I wish everyone a wonderful Games. I trust you'll also have the opportunity to experience the sights, sounds and tastes of Victoria and British Columbia during your stay and may I personally invite you to return in future years to relive memories and enjoy this land we proudly call our home.

Sincerely,

Mike Harcourt
Premier

Province of
British Columbia

Office of the
Premier

Parliament Buildings
Victoria, British Columbia
V8V 1X4

Victoria 94
XV Commonwealth Games
August 18 to 28

Minister's Message

*Minister of Agriculture,
David Zirnhelt*

This publication, *A Celebration of British Columbia Food*, has been prepared to honour the year of XV Commonwealth Games in Victoria and the 100th year of service of the Ministry of Agriculture, Fisheries and Food. To help celebrate this special year, the industry and the Ministry have prepared this showcase to feature the excellent foods and beautiful landscape of our province, British Columbia.

In 1894, the first Department of Agriculture was formed to support and serve the developing industry. Since that time, the mandate has expanded to include fisheries and the food industry. Dramatic changes and advances in technology, production and marketing have made British Columbia's products well-known in the global marketplace. Today, the agri-food industry is highly sophisticated and diversified, with over 200 commodities now being produced.

I am proud of the wide diversity and abundance of food products available from our local agriculture, fisheries and food industries. Furthermore, the dedication and commitment of the over 200,000 British Columbians employed in these industries is worthy of special recognition. British Columbia produces some of the highest quality food and beverages found anywhere in the world.

A Celebration of British Columbia Foods is a fine reflection of much of what is unique to British Columbians. From the rugged coast to the lush valleys and towering mountain peaks, we are fortunate to be able to share with the rest of the world what is special to us. I hope you will enjoy this book and share it with your visitors from around the world.

Sincerely,

David Zirnhelt

David Zirnhelt
Minister

Province of
British Columbia

Minister of
Agriculture, Fisheries
and Food

Parliament Buildings
Victoria, British Columbia V8V 1X4
Telephone: (604) 387-1023
Fax: (604) 387-1522

The Coast

Agriculture, Fish & Food Industry in British Columbia

Super natural British Columbia is well known around the world for the variety and abundance of its one million square kilometres of spectacular scenery. Those same two qualities – variety and abundance – are what distinguishes cooking in British Columbia. By taking advantage of this bounty, the Province's chefs and cooks have created a distinctive west coast cuisine.

West coast cuisine is tied very closely to the land; indeed cooking in British Columbia is a reflection of our geography. The Pacific Ocean offers a world class variety of seafoods that are often front and centre in any menu. The Province's majestic mountains offer up wilderness areas providing fish and game that cannot be equaled; while plateaus are home to vast cattle ranges producing top-quality beef. Some of the Province's smallest areas have the largest impact on cooking in British Columbia. Fertile valley regions that consist of only 5% of the land yield a magnificent harvest of fruits and vegetables that are enjoyed here and around the world. British Columbia boasts an incredible wealth of food, with more foods available here than anywhere else in Canada.

Native heritage plays a significant role in cooking in British Columbia. The First Nations people have carefully maintained their plant and animal resources for centuries through traditional practices and hereditary ownership. They have discovered some of the best ways to enjoy the natural bounty of the land and sea.

British Columbia's position on the coast has also resulted in ethnic influences on our cooking. Immigrants who have crossed the Pacific have added an Asian influence, just as immigrants from Britain, Europe, the United States and around the world are adding their imprint.

Across the Province one can see that west coast cuisine has come of age. BC producers have some of the highest food quality and safety standards in the world. At Vancouver's Granville Island Market, there is an abundance of exotic fruits and vegetables, organic produce, herbs, fresh seafood and game, reflecting the Province's wealth of food and multicultural heritage. In Victoria, the Gulf Islands, the Okanagan, Cariboo, Kootenays or the Peace River country, visitors will find similar scenes. Ethnic restaurants, delicatessans and specialty bakeries exist in every city and many

BCARS No. 30705.

Mixed farming in the Cowichan Valley circa 1860.

Lighthouse Park,
West Vancouver.

British Columbia towns. Remote resorts and guest ranches develop their own specialty recipes and feature British Columbia foods as a major attraction.

West coast cuisine is augmented by a growing range of distinctive and internationally recognized British Columbia wines – the industry has won awards worldwide – while quality ales and lagers are brewed in the traditional style by brew-pubs and micro-breweries.

Nature has blessed British Columbia with incredible beauty and bounty. "A Celebration of British Columbia Food" showcases our province's stunning scenery and unique west coast cuisine.

The Coast

Rugged, remote, pristine, and beautiful, British Columbia's 27,000 kilometres of coast are a spectacular combination of bays, coves, fjords, straits, inlets, arms, sounds and islands. Sprawling sandy beaches, rocky coves, forests and mountains are all defining features of the land that provides food for its many inhabitants.

Where the climate is mild, settlers cultivated the land into farm fields. The rich soils of the Fraser River delta and the Saanich Peninsula on Vancouver Island are ideal for intensive market gardening. Other valleys and islands in Vancouver Island's protected lee are suitable for growing fruit and vegetables and for raising dairy cattle and sheep. Where rock rises abruptly from the waterline and trees are crowded to the waves' edge, the forest and ocean provide food. Native ancestors were the first to discover these cold Pacific waters are rich in fish and shellfish, long the northwest coast's sustaining foods.

RBCM Photo.   *School garden, Tolmie School, 1919.*

The first European to reach the Pacific overland from the prairies was Alexander Mackenzie who arrived near present day Bella Coola. His first west coast meal was roast salmon, dried fish eggs and berries. After watching the natives eat hemlock bark cakes sprinkled with salmon oil, he sampled the cakes himself and found them a great delicacy.

Like the native peoples, new settlers took advantage of the sea's bounty. Sole, salmon, halibut, crabs, clams, abalone, scallops and mussels were all available to coastal families. Added to this were the deer and other mammals found in the forest. A report from Prince Rupert at the beginning of this century shows that a substantial meal cost 25 cents and that rows of slaughtered deer shared space in the shops with marine trophies such as a 100-kilogram halibut.

Early settlers cleared patches, planted seeds, developed pastures and imported farm animals. The roughest coastal areas offered little opportunity for farming, but pioneers persevered to survive. They succeeded best in protected coastal areas where the landscape softened and the land was level. Within three years of the founding of Fort Victoria in 1843, the cleared land yielded wheat, oats, potatoes, carrots, turnips and peas. Meanwhile 70 cows provided the Fort with milk and butter.

The fur trade, the gold rush and Victoria's position as an early west coast port attracted people of many backgrounds – British, Chinese, German, French, West Indian, American and Italian are just a few of the many diverse ethnic groups that made their way to the coast. The culinary needs of naval personnel, entrepreneurs, gold seekers, merchants and labourers, all influenced local cooking styles which in turn utilized the abundance of natural products.

The farming industry grew from its fur trade beginnings to its major presence today on southern Vancouver Island. The tidy fields of the Saanich Peninsula are home to fruit and vegetable growing. Traditional crops such as carrots, lettuce, cabbage, squash, peas and beans have been supplemented by Chinese greens, herbs and some of the world's tastiest green asparagus. Hectares of kiwi fruit vines can be seen alongside strawberry plants, raspberry canes and apple and peach trees. Organic farming is becoming very popular both for home market gardens and commercial operations.

Up-island, in the Cowichan and Comox valleys, the scene is much the same. Dairy cows graze in the valleys, while roadside stands testify to the abundance of farm produce. North of Qualicum, numerous seafood stands provide visitors with the opportunity to stock up on fresh oysters within sight of the huge shell piles accumulated during the harvest.

Between Vancouver Island and the mainland, lie the Gulf Islands. Salt Spring, the largest and most populated island, boasts the famous Salt Spring lamb. Since the turn of the century the island's mineral rich grasses and wild herbs have given the lamb its distinctive flavour, and it is often featured

Cathedral Grove Forest, Port Alberni.

in many B.C. restaurants. Neighbouring Saturna Island hosts an annual lamb barbecue that attracts hundreds of boaters and ferry passengers.

The Gulf Islands provide both wild and cultivated treats. In late summer, a few minutes among blackberry bushes will yield enough sun-warmed fruit for dessert, and an hour's picking provides the basis for pies or jam. With luck, a visitor will find tiny wild strawberries, whose taste recalls William Butler's comment, "Doubtless God could have made a better berry, but doubtless God never did."

As a seaport, Vancouver has drawn people from around the world, many bringing their own unique ways of flavouring and cooking seafood and other dishes. This immigrant legacy influences how Vancouverites prepare their food. Shoppers in the city's Chinatown can choose from gai lan, bok choy, coriander and a dozen other varieties of greens that have been grown on the banks of the Fraser River for generations. To the south, shoppers can stroll Main street at one end for Italian ingredients, at the other for the cumin, pepper, lentils, and other fixings that give East Indian food its distinctive taste. Further west, markets offer olives, feta cheese and other Greek delicacies. Downtown, those planning a Japanese meal can find daikon, rice noodles and sushi. Even government-run liquor stores stock such imports as sake, plum wine and Thai beer. Granville Island Market offers a tremendous assortment of fresh fruits and vegetables, many of which are organically grown.

With its fresh ingredients, wild and cultivated, and its multicultural culinary traditions, the coast provides ample opportunity for sampling the best of British Columbia's cuisine.

Fishing pier at Campbell River.

Windsurfing off Beacon Hill Park.

Zesty Pacific Salmon Steaks

The zip of cayenne and the zest of lemon juice make simple pan-fried salmon spectacularly good. Fresh salmon is in season July to September. Today's frozen salmon is also excellent.

4	Pacific salmon steaks about 1-inch (2.5 cm) thick	4
	pinch of cayenne for each steak	
2	garlic cloves, crushed	2
2 tbsp.	olive oil	30 mL
⅓ cup	fresh parsley or dill, chopped	75 mL
1 tsp.	capers	5 mL
1 tsp	lemon zest	5 mL
¼ cup	lemon juice	50 mL

Sprinkle salmon steaks with cayenne. Sauté 1 clove garlic in oil at medium heat until golden; remove from oil. Increase heat to medium-high. Sauté salmon 4 minutes on each side. Add remaining clove of garlic, parsley, capers, lemon zest and lemon juice. Cook 1 to 2 minutes longer. Serve drizzled with pan juices. MAKES 4 SERVINGS.

Per Serving: Protein 40.3 g; Fat 16.1 g; Carbohydrate 2.4 g; Kilocalories 311.5; Kilojoules 1303.3; Potassium 762.4 mg; Sodium 160.5 mg; Calcium 85.9 mg.

The nutritional breakdown of this recipe falls within the criteria for the Heart Smart Restaurant Program.

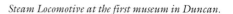
Steam Locomotive at the first museum in Duncan.

Nanaimo Bars

½ cup	butter	125 mL
¼ cup	granulated sugar	50 mL
¼ cup	cocoa	50 mL
1 tsp.	vanilla	5 mL
1	egg, beaten	1
2 cups	graham wafer crumbs	500 mL
⅓ cup	finely chopped nuts	75 mL
1 cup	coconut	250 mL
¼ cup	butter	50 mL
3 tbsp.	milk	45 mL
3 tbsp.	vanilla custard powder	45 mL
2 cups	sifted icing sugar	500 mL
4	squares semi-sweet chocolate (1 oz./28 g) each	4
1 tbsp.	butter	15 mL

Mix ½ cup (125 mL) butter, granulated sugar, cocoa, vanilla and egg in the top of a double boiler. Heat over hot, not boiling, water until butter melts and mixture thickens slightly. Mix graham wafer crumbs, nuts and coconut. Add cocoa mixture and stir until well-mixed. Pat onto bottom of a lightly-greased 9-inch (23 cm) baking pan. Chill. Beat together ¼ cup (50 mL) butter, milk, custard powder and icing sugar until smooth. Pour over cocoa layer in pan. Chill until firm. Melt semi-sweet chocolate and 1 tbsp. (15 mL) butter in a double boiler over hot water. Cool slightly and spread over custard layer. Chill until firm. Cut in squares. MAKES 30 SQUARES.

Historic Bastion in Nanaimo. *Tulips at Ladysmith.*

Orca breaching in the Johnstone Straits.

Barbecued Salmon with Blueberry Salsa

The best of the West Coast. Fresh salmon is in season July - September. Today's frozen salmon is also excellent.

1	Pacific salmon fillet, 1½ lbs./750 g	1
Blueberry Salsa		
½	large pink grapefruit	½
2 tbsp.	red onion, finely chopped	25 mL
1	chopped jalapeño pepper	1
1 tsp.	honey	5 mL
1 tbsp.	lime juice	15 mL
1 cup	blueberries, fresh or thawed	250 mL
2 tbsp.	chopped fresh cilantro	30 mL

Section pink grapefruit and discard membrane. Dice grapefruit and mix with other salsa ingredients. Prepare the barbecue and oil the grill well. Cut the salmon into 4 serving portions. Barbecue skin-side down over medium high heat for about 10 minutes per inch of thickness. Spoon salsa over the salmon or serve on the side. MAKES 4 SERVINGS.

Per Serving: Protein 38.0 g; Fat 8.8 g; Carbohydrate 10.0 g; Kilocalories 265.8; Kilojoules 1112.1; Sodium 141.2 mg; Calcium 89.1 mg; Potassium 751.2 mg.

The nutritional breakdown of this recipe falls within the criteria for the Heart Smart Restaurant Program.

Prawns.

Anacortes Ferry leaving Sidney.

Exploring at Sidney Spit.

Sealife watching at Bamfield.

Pachena Oven Poached Sole

1 lb.	sole fillets	500 g
3 tbsp.	butter	45 mL
1½ cups	sliced mushrooms	375 mL
3 tbsp.	minced green onions	45 mL
½ tsp.	salt	2 mL
	pepper to taste	
¼ cup	dry white wine	50 mL
	lemon wedges	

Arrange fillets in a lightly greased baking dish. Melt butter in a small skillet at medium heat. Add mushrooms and onions; sauté until soft but not brown. Add salt and pepper to taste. Spread mushroom mixture over fillets; pour wine over top. Bake, covered, at 425°F (220°C) for 15 to 20 minutes until fish flakes easily. Garnish with lemon wedges. 4 SERVINGS.

Per Serving: Protein 27.7 g; Fat 11.5 g; Carbohydrate 50 g; Kilocalories 428; Potassium 863.8 mg; Sodium 820 mg.

The Pachena Oven Poached Sole served with 1/2 cup (125 mL) plain rice and a plain vegetable – e.g. asparagus 1/2 cup (125 mL) – meets Heart Smart criteria. Only 1/2 tsp. (2 mL) or less of salt should be added for flavour.

The nutritional breakdown of this recipe falls within the criteria for the Heart Smart Restaurant Program.

Heart Smart

Blueberry Relish

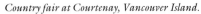

3 cups	blueberries	750 mL
1	apple, peeled and diced	1
½ cup	sugar	125 mL
1	whole cinnamon stick	1
1 tsp.	whole cloves	5 mL
2 tsp.	vinegar	10 mL
4 tsp.	lemon juice	20 mL

In large saucepan, combine blueberries, apple, sugar, cinnamon and cloves. Bring to a boil; reduce heat and simmer for 3 minutes. Add vinegar and lemon juice. Stir carefully just to mix. Remove from heat and let cool. Pour through large strainer to drain off juice. Remove cinnamon and cloves. Chill the mixture. YIELD: 1½ CUPS.

Blueberries.

Country fair at Courtenay, Vancouver Island.

Steveston Shrimp Curry

2 tbsp.	butter	25 mL
¼ cup	finely chopped onion	50 mL
3 tbsp.	finely chopped green pepper	45 mL
3 tbsp.	finely chopped celery	45 mL
3 tbsp.	flour	45 mL
1 tsp.	curry powder (or to taste)	5 mL
1	chicken bouillon cube, crushed	1
2 cups	milk	500 mL
3 cups	cooked shrimp	750 mL
	hot cooked rice	

In a large saucepan at medium heat, melt butter. Add onion, green pepper and celery. Cook until soft but not brown. Blend in flour, curry powder, and chicken bouillon cube. Gradually add milk. Cook and stir until thick. Stir in shrimp. Continue to cook and stir until shrimp is heated. Serve immediately over rice. 4 TO 6 SERVINGS.

Selling shellfish.

Fishing boats at Steveston.

Deep-Fried Ginseng

	several fresh ginseng roots, cleaned	
Batter:		
½ cup	all-purpose flour	125 mL
¼ cup	cornstarch	50 mL
1	egg	1
	dash salt	
¼ tsp.	baking powder	2 mL
½ - ¾ cup	water	125 - 175 mL
	oil for deep-frying	
Dipping Sauce:		
1 tbsp.	soy sauce	15 mL
1 tbsp.	sherry	15 mL
¼ tsp.	vinegar	1 mL
¼ tsp.	sugar	1 mL

Pound the cleaned ginseng roots lightly and cut them in half or quarter lengthwise.

Prepare the batter by combining flour, cornstarch, egg, salt, baking powder and water.

Coat the ginseng slices with batter.

Deep-fry over medium heat.

Blend together soy sauce, sherry, vinegar and sugar to make Dipping Sauce. Serve "Deep-Fried Ginseng" with Dipping Sauce.

Celebration Cookies

…perfect for decorating or just as they are!

1⅔ cups	no-additive/all-purpose flour	400 mL
1½ tsp.	baking powder	7 mL
½ tsp.	salt	2 mL
½ cup	quick cooking oats	125 mL
¾ cup	margarine	175 mL
¾ cup	sugar	175 mL
1	egg	1
2 tsp.	grated lemon rind	10 mL

Combine no-additive/all-purpose flour, baking powder, salt and oats and stir well. Cream margarine and sugar together; add egg and grated lemon rind and beat well. Gradually add flour mixture to the creamed mixture, stirring well after each addition. Chill dough.

Preheat oven to 375°F (190°C). On lightly floured board, roll out chilled dough to ⅛-inch (3 mm) thickness. Cut dough into cookies using any shaped or round cookie cutters. Place cookies on prepared baking sheets and bake for 10 minutes or until slightly browned. Cool on rack. Decorate if desired.   MAKES 30 TO 40 COOKIES.

Shrimp and fresh produce, perfect for a stir-fry.

Rathtrevor Beach.

Stanley Park, Vancouver.

Salt Spring Island Leg of Lamb

1	leg of lamb (5 lbs./2.5 kg)	1
½ tsp.	rosemary leaves	2 mL
	dash pepper	
1 cup	dry white wine	250 mL
2 tbsp.	brown sugar	30 mL
1 tbsp.	flour	15 mL
¼ tsp.	nutmeg	1 mL
2 tbsp.	lemon juice	30 mL
½ cup	water	125 mL
1	can (14 oz./398 mL)	
	whole cranberry sauce	1

Slash fat on leg of lamb. Place lamb on a rack in large roasting pan. Rub rosemary and pepper into slashes on lamb. Pour wine over. Insert meat thermometer into lamb, not touching fat or bone. Roast, uncovered, at 325°F (160°C) until thermometer registers 160°F (70°C) about 2½ hours. Meanwhile, mix remaining ingredients in a small saucepan. Place over low heat until cranberry sauce melts. Baste lamb with this sauce frequently during last hour of cooking. MAKES 8 SERVINGS.

Heart Smart

Per Serving (120g): Protein 36.87g; Fat 9.04 g; Carbohydrate 27.05g; Kilocalories 362.74; Potassium 465.55mg; Sodium 109.97 mg.

The nutritional breakdown of this recipe falls within the criteria for the Heart Smart Restaurant Program.

Strawberry Glazed Pie

1	package (1 oz. 7g)	
	unglavored gelatin	1
¼ cup	cold water	50 mL
4 cups	sliced strawberries	1 L
1 cup	water	250 mL
1 cup	sugar	250 mL
1	baked pastry shell (8-inch/20 cm)	1
	sweetened whipped	
	whipping cream (optional)	

Soak gelatin in cold water. Cook 1 cup (250 mL) strawberries in 1 cup (250 mL) water until soft. Strain. Add sugar and gelatin to hot liquid and stir until dissolved. Let chill until the consistency of egg white. Fold in remaining 3 cups (750 mL) of berries. Pour into baked pastry shell. Chill until firm. Serve with sweetened whipped whipping cream if desired.

North of Campbell River, Vancouver Island.

Rebecca Spit on Quadra Island.

Flowers along a fence in Courtenay.

Chemainus Speedy Stroganoff

½ lb.	turkey stir-fry strips or turkey breast, cut into thin strips	250 g
2 tsp.	butter or margarine	10 mL
1	onion, minced	1
8	fresh mushrooms, sliced	8
½ cup	light sour cream	125 mL
2 tbsp.	sherry	30 mL
	salt and pepper to taste	
	ground nutmeg	

Stir-fry onions and mushrooms in butter in a non-stick skillet until onions are limp. Add turkey and cook until pink colour has disappeared. Mix sour cream and sherry until smooth. Stir into the turkey mixture. Heat but do NOT allow to boil. Add salt and pepper. Garnish with nutmeg. Serve as is or over pasta. MAKES 2 SERVINGS.

Per Serving: Kilocalories 291.61; Fat 13.94 g; Sodium 198.37 mg; Protein 33.02 g; Carbohydrate 8.42 g; Potassium 789.54 mg.

The nutritional breakdown of this recipe falls within the criteria for the Heart Smart Restaurant Program.

Chemainus.

Rhododendrons.

Berries.

Abbotsford Raspberry Cloud

6	egg whites	6
	dash salt	
½ tsp.	cream of tartar	2 mL
1 cup	sugar	250 mL
1 tsp.	vanilla	5 mL
2 cups	whipping cream	500 mL
3 tbsp.	sugar	45 mL
3 cups	fresh raspberries	750 mL

Line a large cookie sheet with brown paper. Draw a 10-inch (25 cm) circle in centre. Preheat oven to 400°F (200°C). In a large bowl, beat egg whites, salt, cream of tartar until soft peaks form. Continue beating, gradually adding 1 cup (250 mL) sugar, 1 tablespoonful (15 mL) at a time, until meringue is stiff and glossy. Beat in vanilla. Using a large pastry bag, pipe meringue onto circle drawn on brown paper, making edges higher than centre. Place in oven; turn off heat and let stand in oven overnight. Keep oven door closed. To serve, loosen meringue with a spatula and slide onto a serving dish. Whip cream until thick, gradually adding the 3 tbsp. (45 mL) sugar. Fill meringue shell with berries, saving a few for garnish. Spread sweetened whipped cream over top and garnish with reserved berries. Serve immediately. 10 SERVINGS.

Farm near Koksilah.

Rathtrevor Provincial Park near Parksville.

Oak Bay Honey Nut Sundaes

1 tbsp.	instant coffee	15 mL
2 tbsp.	boiling water	30 mL
½ cup	liquid honey	125 mL
¼ cup	chopped filberts or pecans	50 mL
2 cups	ice cream	500 mL

Dissolve instant coffee in boiling water. Stir into honey. Add nuts and mix until well-combined. Place scoops of ice cream in serving dishes – use coffee, chocolate, or vanilla flavours. Pour sauce over ice cream and serve immediately. 4 SERVINGS.

Parliament Buildings, Victoria.

Bengal Curry

2 tbsp.	butter	30 mL
1	large garlic clove, minced	1
1	large onion, sliced	1
1½ tbsp.	curry powder (mild)	20 mL
3 lbs.	chicken thighs, skinned	1.5 kg
1	can (19 oz./540 mL) tomatoes	1
2 tbsp.	tomato paste	30 mL
½ cup	sultana raisins	125 mL
2	apples, peeled and cubed	2
2 tbsp.	lime juice	30 mL
1	bay leaf	1
	pinch sugar	
2 tbsp.	fresh coriander, chopped	30 mL
	salt and pepper	
Garnish:		
4 cups	steamed rice	1000 mL
	unsweetened grated coconut	
½ cup	toasted almonds	125 mL
	or	
½	pineapple, cubed	½

In a 12-cup (3 L) microwave-safe casserole, melt butter 45 seconds on HIGH. Add garlic, onion; cook 2 minutes, uncovered also at HIGH power. Stir and add curry powder. Cook for 1 minute on HIGH. Stir well and add chicken pieces. Cook for 5 minutes on HIGH power. Cover with waxed paper. Turn chicken pieces over.

Mix tomatoes with tomato paste and blend in remaining ingredients, except for the coriander and garnish.

Cook for 15 minutes at HIGH power, covered with waxed paper. Stir once during cooking time. Add the fresh coriander and cook 1 more minute. Sprinkle with salt and pepper. Let stand for 5 minutes. Serve chicken on a heated serving platter over plain rice. Sprinkle with grated coconut; arrange toasted almonds and fruit cubes in a circle around chicken as garnish. MAKES 4 SERVINGS.

Per Serving: Protein 68.3 g; Fat 19.5 g; Carbohydrate 105.8 g; Kilocalories 857.2; kilojoules 3586.5; Potassium 1726.5 mg; Sodium 766.7 mg.

The nutritional breakdown of this recipe falls within the criteria for the Heart Smart Restaurant Program.

Totem Park at the Provincial Museum in Victoria.

Clam Patties

As given by Beverly Antoine, Head Cook,
Native Heritage Centre in Duncan, BC.

1 quart	razor clams	1 L
1	small onion, diced	1
1	each small red and green pepper, diced	1
1 tbsp.	baking powder	15 mL
1 tbsp.	curry powder	15 mL
3	eggs	3
2 cups	flour	500 mL

Dice clams into small pieces. Add onion and peppers. Add remaining ingredients. Mix well. Spoon into hot oil or lard and fry until golden. Drain on paper towels and serve hot.
MAKES APPROXIMATELY 80 - 1 OZ. PORTIONS.

Soapalali Berries "Indian Ice Cream"

Grows plentiful in British Columbia. Ripens in July.

	Soapalali berries	
¼ cup	water	50 mL
	sugar	

Squeeze enough juice from berries to make ½ cup juice. Put in mixer and add ¼ cup water. Mix at high speed until very stiff. While mixing, add sugar to taste. Aboriginal women mixed "Indian Ice Cream" by hand when there were no mixers or electricity.

Saanich Peninsula from the Malahat Lookout.

Devilled Oysters

2 cups	oysters, undrained	500 mL
2 tbsp.	butter	25 mL
½ cup	chopped onion	125 mL
⅓ cup	chopped celery	75 mL
½ cup	cracker crumbs	125 mL
1 tbsp.	Worcestershire sauce	15 mL
1 tbsp.	chopped parsley	15 mL
1 tbsp.	catsup	15 mL
	juice of ½ a small lemon	
	dash tabasco	
	salt and pepper to taste	
⅓ cup	dry bread crumbs	75 mL
1 tbsp.	butter, melted	15 mL
	lemon twists, parsley sprigs and tomato wedges	

Place oysters in saucepan; heat oysters in their own juices just until the edges curl. Remove from heat. Using a slotted spoon, remove oysters from saucepan, leaving juices; set oysters aside. Meanwhile, in small skillet, in 2 tbsp. (25 mL) butter, cook onion and celery just until tender. To oyster juices in saucepan, add sautéed onion mixture, cracker crumbs, Worcestershire sauce, parsley, catsup, lemon juice, and tabasco. Season to taste with salt and pepper. Stir well to distribute seasonings. Add oysters. Gently stir. Turn mixture into buttered casserole dish. Stir together bread crumbs and 1 tbsp. (15 mL) melted butter. Sprinkle over oyster mixture. Bake in 425°F (220°C) oven for 10 to 15 minutes – just until oysters are sizzling but not dry. Garnish with lemon twists, parsley sprigs and tomato wedges. MAKES 4 TO 6 SERVINGS.

Valleys & Plains

Almost all of British Columbia's supply of agricultural land falls within its valleys and plains. Three major areas – the Fraser Valley, the Okanagan Valley and the Peace River country account for most of the Province's produce and livestock.

The Fraser Valley is the broadest of the river valleys. For much of its 5,100 kilometre length, the Fraser River is turbulent and constricted between steep rocky banks, tree-clad hills or dry terraces. Forced westward at Hope by a mountain barrier, the Fraser rolls out into the wide valley that leads to Vancouver and the sea. Over thousands of years the river has deposited silt to form a fertile delta where more than half the agricultural products of the Province are grown or raised.

The Fraser Valley was the scene of the first commercial food production in British Columbia. In 1827, James McMillan of the Hudson's Bay Company established Fort Langley on the banks of the Fraser River which maintained a farm of 2,000 acres. The crops produced helped provision coastal fur trading ships and feed the fort's inhabitants. In addition the fort employed Native workers in the production of barrels of salt salmon for export to such exotic locales as Hawaii, Peru and China.

Today, the Fraser Valley is a patchwork of fields that fill each summer with ripening corn, cabbages, broccoli, cauliflower, beans, peppers, zucchini, spinach, chard, Chinese green vegetables, radishes and carrots. Locally grown, aromatic hops, their long vines supported by distinctive aerial trellises, have long been supplied to Canadian breweries. The Valley also contributes fresh fruit to the Province's markets. Abbotsford styles itself as the raspberry capital of the world and few who sample the berries would contest that claim.

White farmhouses and trim red barns in green pastures near Chilliwack testify to the success of another type of agriculture, dairying. The dairy industry started here in 1885 when A. C. Wells opened a creamery, the valley's first. Wells' wife named the creamery Edensbank, thinking that no place could be closer to the Garden of Eden than the farmland beside Katzie Slough.

East of the Fraser Valley is the Okanagan Valley. While the Fraser, watered by heavy rain clouds trapped by the Cascade Mountains, is lush and green, the Okanagan has another climate altogether. It lies in the rain shadow of the Cascades, receiving just 30 to 40 centimetres of precipitation each year. Without irrigation, the hillsides that rise above the long lakes in the centre of the valley support only sagebrush, pines and cacti. Yet the soil in the valley bottom is fertile. Ten thousand years ago receding glaciers left deposits of gravel and silt that has eroded to form alluvial fans and deltas beside the lakes.

Irishman Thomas Ellis, who settled in the Penticton area in 1866, began commercial apple production in the Okanagan. Ellis was the first non-native to claim land between Okanagan and Skaha lakes, an area the Salish called *phthanuntauc* ("place to stay forever"). Ellis and his wife Wilhemina stayed, raised nine children, planted apple trees and expanded their ranch to 12,000 hectares.

Others also saw the potential of the valley. Lord Aberdeen, Canada's Governor-General in the late nineteenth century, had large property

BCARS No. 22461.   *Apple pickers near Kelowna.*

Fraser Valley, near Chilliwack.

holdings in the north Okanagan and encouraged the planting of orchards. Initially, pioneer orchardists had to surmount winter freezing, insects and inadequate irrigation. With the introduction of new varieties and rootstocks, improved technology, and research discoveries in disease and pest control, the orchards and their owners have become an important part of British Columbia's agricultural industry.

Aided by irrigation waters drawn from the lakes and blessed with 2,000 hours of sunshine a year, the terraces of the Okanagan are ideal for tree-fruit growing. In Spring, the pink and white petals of fruit trees transform the valley. Each summer, visitors make their way across the Okanagan valley, visiting farms and roadside stands in search of the freshest cherries, peaches, plums, apricots, pears, apples, tomatoes, corn and other produce. Most of the fruit is shipped worldwide in the late summer and fall.

The Okanagan and neighbouring Similkameen Valley compose one of only two areas in Canada where grapes are grown commercially. Wine-making was left to Italian families in Kelowna, led by Guiseppe Ghezzi, who made the first Okanagan wine from surplus apples. Pasquale "Cap" Capozzi and future B.C. premier W.A.C. Bennett were soon involved in the valley's first wineries. From their ventures developed the Calona wines. Today some 1,000 hectares of vineyards supply an assortment of commercial, estate and farm wineries that are gaining international acclaim.

Valley farmers also grow vegetables, raise poultry and eggs, keep bees to produce honey and raise cattle for beef and dairy products. Organic farmers grow a wide variety of produce – small fruits, vegetables, apples, pears and peaches. At the valley's north end, Armstrong produces an aged, piquant cheddar that is a British Columbia favourite.

Eastward across more mountain ranges lie the Creston lowlands. The soils created by glacial erosion in this flat bottomed valley yield superb fruits and vegetables. Creston is the centre of southeast farmland, with the Grand Forks area

Okanagan Valley.

to the west also supporting commercial farming. Local potatoes and beets go into the borscht made by the descendants of Doukhobors who settled this region early in the century.

Only one corner of British Columbia lies east of the Rockies, tied more by terrain and temperment to Alberta and the prairies. The southernmost part is British Columbia's only true plains. Alexander Mackenzie's lyrical 18th-century description of Peace River country still strikes a chord, "This magnificent theatre of nature has all the decorations which the trees and animals of the country can afford it: groves of poplar in every shape vary the scene; and their intervals are enlivened with vast herds of elk and buffaloes". The buffalo are gone, but the lofty poplars still add texture to the furrowed fields of this region that is almost as large as Great Britain.

Early settlers found the Peace to be a hunter's paradise and filled their larders with moose, bear and beaver, as well as many types of fish. Pioneer gardeners reported growing onions, carrots, potatoes, tomatoes, pumpkins, cucumbers,

squash and rhubarb. In 1873 railway surveyor Charles Horetztky predicted the Peace River's future. It would be, he suggested, the future garden of the west, for even without cultivation, it was "replete with the finest wild fruits peculiar to both woods and plains," and had the choicest soil on the continent.

Farmers have now brought close to a half-million hectares in the Peace River region under cultivation. The rich, black soil produces most of the Province's grain and forage crops, pastureland supports beef cattle and sheep, and bees collect the nectar from abundant wildflowers to produce the famous Peace River honey.

The Government, through the Agricultural Land Reserve, has made a commitment to preserve food lands for future generations. British Columbia's valleys and plains, though a relatively small portion of the Province's land, offer an abundance of fruit, vegetables and other fresh foods that are enthusiastically incorporated into dishes in the kitchens of the Province.

Ginger Turkey Stir-Fry

½ lb.	turkey thigh, boneless and skinless or turkey breast	250 g
1 tbsp.	dry white wine	15 mL
2 tsp.	soy sauce	10 mL
½ cup	water	125 mL
2 tsp.	cornstarch	10 mL
2 tsp.	vegetable oil	10 mL
1	garlic clove, minced	1
2 tsp.	fresh ginger, minced	10 mL
3 cups	thinly sliced vegetables (carrots, celery, zucchini, mushrooms, green or red peppers)	750 mL
1	green onion, sliced steamed rice or rice noodles	1

Member of 4-H Club.

Cut turkey into bite-sized pieces. In medium bowl, combine turkey, wine and 1 tsp. (5 mL) soy sauce. Set aside. In small bowl, combine water, remaining soy sauce and cornstarch. Set aside. In a wok or large frying pan, stir-fry turkey until no pink remains. Remove turkey from wok. Add oil to wok and stir-fry garlic, ginger and vegetables until tender. Add green onion and stir-fry for 1 minute. Stir in turkey and add cornstarch mixture. Cook, stirring constantly, until thickened. Serve with steamed rice or rice noodles. MAKES 2 SERVINGS.

Per Serving: Protein 14.88 g; Fat 6.17 g; Carbohydrate 39.55 g; Kilocalories 256.91; Potassium 583.95 mg; Sodium 314.29 mg.

The nutritional breakdown of this recipe falls within the criteria for the Heart Smart Restaurant Program.

Family picnic.

Freezer-to-Table Steak with Pistou

Recommended BC Wine: Kelowna Rougeon.
Preparation time: 10 minutes. Cooking time: 10 minutes.
Here's a rush-hour meal for unexpected company. Spread frozen steak with a wonderful herb-cheese combination and pop it straight under the broiler. Serve with linguine or boiled new potatoes and steamed green beans.

Pistou:

5	garlic cloves, finely chopped	5
1 cup	fresh basil	250 mL
	(or ¼ cup/50 mL dried)	
1 cup	freshly grated Parmesan cheese	250 mL
3 tbsp.	tomato paste	45 mL
½ cup	olive oil	125 mL

Meat:

4	frozen strip loin or rib-eye	4
	steaks (4 oz./125 g) each	
¼ cup	Pistou	50 mL

In a bowl, pound garlic and basil into a paste. Work in Parmesan and tomato paste; beat in olive oil, 1 tbsp. (15 mL) at a time. The Pistou will keep indefinitely in a jar in the refrigerator. Makes 1½ cups (375 mL).

Brush steak on both sides with Pistou. Broil or grill over hot coals or at high setting on a gas barbecue for 4 to 5 minutes on each side for rare meat; 5 to 7 minutes per side for medium. MAKES 4 SERVINGS.

Per Serving: Energy 239 Calories; Fat 13 g; Sodium 117 mg; 1000 kilojoules; Protein 29 g; Potassium 404 mg.

The nutritional breakdown of this recipe falls within the criteria for the Heart Smart Restaurant Program.

Tulip field at Abbotsford.

Cayoosh Creek, Cariboo Shuswap area.

Fraser Valley Vegetable Medley

1½ cups	cauliflower florets	375 mL
1½ cups	cups broccoli florets	375 mL
1 cup	chopped carrots	250 mL
1 cup	chopped rutabaga	250 mL
¼ cup	vinegar	50 mL
2 tbsp.	cooking oil	30 mL
1 tbsp.	sugar	15 mL
½ tsp.	salt	2 mL
¼ tsp.	pepper	1 mL
¼ tsp	dry mustard	1 mL
¼ tsp.	thyme	1 mL
¼ tsp.	oregano	1 mL
	minced parsley	

Cook vegetables in boiling water until crisp-tender. Drain well and place in a large bowl. Combine remaining ingredients except parsley. Pour over vegetables. Refrigerate several hours or overnight, stirring occasionally. Just before serving, sprinkle with parsley. 4 TO 6 SERVINGS.

The amount of cooking oil used in this recipe can be increased up to ½ cup (125 mL) if desired. The recipe does not fit into the Heart Smart guidelines when more than 2 tbsp. (30 mL) oil is used.

Per Serving: Protein 1.7 g; Fat 4.8 g; Carbohydrate 8.2 g; Kilocalories 76; Potassium 316 mg; Sodium 180 mg.

The nutritional breakdown of this recipe falls within the criteria for the Heart Smart Restaurant Program.

Wheat at Keremeos.

Roasted Rutabaga Soup
with Caramelized Onions

Roasted onions and rutabaga gives this creamy Autumn soup a lovely sweet flavour.

Chive Cream:

½ cup	low-fat sour cream	125 mL
⅓ cup	snipped chives	75 mL
	or green onion tops	

Soup:

4	onions	4
3	shallots	3
8	garlic cloves	8
2 lbs.	rutabaga	1 kg
2 tbsp.	olive oil	25 mL
¼ tsp.	each salt and pepper	1 mL
6 cups	chicken or vegetable stock	1.5 L
2 cups	fresh apple juice or cider	500 mL
2 tbsp.	dry sherry (optional)	25 mL
1 tbsp.	each chopped fresh basil	
	and thyme	15 mL
¼ tsp.	nutmeg	1 mL
1	bay leaf	1
	chopped fresh basil for garnish	

Historic Grist Mill at Keremeos.

Chive Cream: in bowl, combine sour cream and chives. (May be covered and refrigerated for 1 day.)

Soup: halve peeled onions and shallots lengthwise; thinly slice. Halve peeled garlic lengthwise. Cut peeled rutabaga into cubes. In large shallow roasting pan, toss vegetables with oil, salt and pepper. Roast, uncovered in 450°F (230°C) oven 1 hour and 15 minutes, stirring every 15 minutes, or until onions are golden. Remove from oven and pour in 1 cup (250 mL) of the stock. Stir, scraping browned bits up on bottom of pan. Transfer onion mixture and juices to large heavy saucepan. Add remaining stock, apple juice, sherry, basil, thyme, nutmeg and bay leaf. Bring to boil; reduce heat to low and simmer, covered 20 minutes. Discard bay leaf. Taste and adjust seasoning.

Purée ¾ of the soup in batches in food processor. Return soup to saucepan; heat through. Ladle soup into bowls. Garnish with dollop of chive cream and fresh basil.

MAKES ABOUT 10 CUPS (2.5 L) SOUP, ENOUGH FOR 6 TO 8 SERVINGS.

Triathlon at Oliver, Okanagan Valley.

Spicy Stir-Fried Pork and Pasta

An outstanding quantity recipe to use for entertaining!

6 lbs.	pork leg, boneless, well-trimmed and cut into strips	2.7 kg
Marinade:		
⅓ cup	Hoisin sauce	75 mL
⅓ cup	soy sauce, low-sodium	75 mL
⅓ cup	dry sherry	75 mL
Sauce:		
5 cups	beef stock, low-sodium	1.25 L
½ cup	dry sherry	125 mL
1 cup	soy sauce, low-sodium	250 mL
¼ cup	Hoisin sauce	50 mL
¼ cup	red wine vinegar	50 mL
1	orange rind, grated	1
2 tsp.	chilies, dried, crushed	10 mL
1 tbsp.	sugar	15 mL
1 tsp.	black pepper	5 mL
4 oz.	cornstarch	113 g
Stir-Fry:		
¼ cup	peanut oil	50 mL
⅛ cup	toasted sesame oil	30 mL
8	garlic cloves, minced	8
2 oz.	ginger, fresh, grated	60 g
12 total	sweet peppers (mix red, green, yellow)	12 total
2 lbs.	mushrooms, quartered	900 g
2	bunches green onions, sliced	2
Pasta:		
3 oz.	fresh herbs, chopped (basil, oregano, parsley)	85 g
4 lbs.	dry pasta* (farfalle, penne, rotini or rigatoni)	1.8 kg

Marinade:

Marinate pork strips in a mixture of Hoisin sauce, soy sauce and sherry for at least 3 hours. Drain and discard marinade.

Sauce:

In large bowl, thoroughly blend all sauce ingredients.

Stir-fry pork strips in both oils about 2 minutes; remove and keep warm. Add garlic and ginger to pan. Stir-fry briefly. Add peppers and mushrooms; stir-fry until crisp-tender, about 5 minutes. Stir sauce thoroughly and add to skillet; stir while bringing to a boil. Add pork and green onions; simmer 5 minutes or until hot.

Cook pasta in unsalted water, keeping very firm. If preparing ahead, rinse with cold water until very cool, drain and refrigerate, covered. To reheat, dip in boiling water briefly. Do not oil pasta. Toss herbs with hot pasta. Serve "Spicy Stir-Fried Pork" over pasta.

Per Serving (Stir-Fry 310 g/11 oz., Pasta (170 g/6 oz.): Energy 524 calories/2190 kj; Protein 36.6 g; Fat 8.7 g; Carbohydrate 72.5 g; Cholesterol 63 g; Sodium 604 mg; Potassium 890 mg.

The nutritional breakdown of this recipe falls within the criteria for the Heart Smart Restaurant Program.

Triathlon athletes in Penticton, Okanagan Valley.

*Spring blossoms
at Mission.*

Sour Cream Apple Pie

4	medium apples	4
½ cup	sugar, divided	125 mL
2 tbsp.	flour	25 mL
¼ tsp.	cinnamon	1 mL
¼ tsp.	ground cloves	1 mL
1	unbaked pie shell (9-inch/23 cm)	1
2	eggs	2
1½ cups	sour cream	375 mL
½ tsp.	vanilla	2 mL
	cinnamon	

Peel, core and slice apples. Toss with ¼ cup (50 mL) sugar, flour, cinnamon and cloves. Arrange in pie shell. Beat eggs lightly. Add ¼ cup (50 mL) sugar, sour cream and vanilla. Beat until smooth. Pour over apples. Sprinkle lightly with cinnamon. Bake at 400°F (200°C) for 12 minutes; reduce oven to 350°F (180°C) and bake about 40 minutes longer until apples are tender and filling is set. 6 TO 8 SERVINGS.

Cherry Coffee Cake

1	egg, beaten	1
½ cup	granulated sugar	125 mL
1½ cups	flour	375 mL
2 tsp.	baking powder	10 mL
½ tsp.	cinnamon	2 mL
	dash salt	
⅓ cup	milk	75 mL
3 tbsp.	melted butter	45 mL
1 tsp.	vanilla	5 mL
1 cup	chopped pitted cherries	250 mL
2 tbsp.	brown sugar	25 mL

Beat together egg and granulated sugar until smooth. Sift together flour, baking powder, cinnamon and salt. Mix together milk, melted butter and vanilla. Add dry ingredients to egg mixture alternately with liquid ingredients. Beat well after each addition. Fold in cherries. Pour into a lightly-greased 9-inch (23 cm) round baking pan. Sprinkle brown sugar over top of cake. Bake at 375°F (190°C) for 25 to 30 minutes. Serve warm. 12 SERVINGS.

Spartan apples in the Okanagan Valley.

*Lake Okanagan
at Summerland.*

Picking grapes.

Okanagan Grape Pie

1	pastry for double-crust pie	1
1 cup	sugar	250 mL
1 tbsp.	all-purpose flour	15 mL
2½ cups	Coronation blue grapes	625 mL
1 tsp.	butter	5 mL

Prepare your favourite pastry recipe and line 1 pie plate. Mix sugar and flour together. Add Coronation blue grapes and turn into pie plate. Top with butter and cover with pastry. Make slits in top of pastry to allow steam to vent. Bake in a 375°F (190°C) oven for 1 hour or until done.

Osoyoos cherries.

Orchards on Lake Okanagan, north of Summerland.

Penticton Brandied Peaches

½ cup	water	125 mL
½ cup	sugar	125 mL
4	medium peaches, peeled and sliced	4
2 tbsp.	brandy	25 mL
1 tsp.	vanilla	5 mL
	dash cinnamon	
	vanilla ice cream	

In a large skillet at medium-high heat, bring water and sugar to boiling, stirring often. Add peaches. Reduce heat and simmer, covered, for about 10 minutes until tender, stirring often. Remove from heat; stir in brandy, vanilla, and cinnamon. Chill. To serve, spoon peaches and their sauce into dishes and top with scoops of ice cream. 4 SERVINGS.

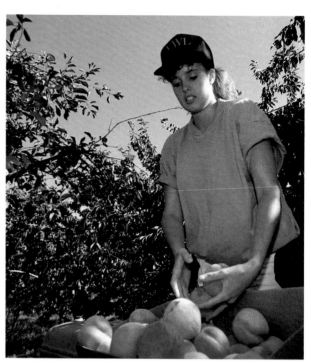

Peach harvest.

MacIntosh apples, Okanagan Valley.

Park land at White Lake.

Beach at Ellison Provincial Park.

Vernon Chicken Salad in Tomato Cups

2 cups	diced cooked chicken	500 mL
1 cup	diced red apple with peel	250 mL
2 cups	finely shredded cabbage	500 mL
3 tbsp.	mayonnaise	45 mL
3 tbsp.	minced parsley	45 mL
1 tbsp.	caraway seed	15 mL
1/2 tsp.	celery salt	2 mL
6	large firm tomatoes	6

Combine all ingredients except tomatoes and chill well (at least 1 hour). Cut tops off tomatoes. Scoop out pulp leaving enough wall to remain firm. Discard pulp or save for use in other recipes. Turn upside down and drain well. Fill with chilled ingredients and serve. MAKES 6 SERVINGS.

Note: It may be necessary to cut a thin slice off bottom of tomatoes to make them stand upright.

Heart Smart

Per Serving: Protein 10.5 g; Fat 5.0 g; Carbohydrate 19.0 g; Kilocalories 153.1; Kilojoules 640.6; Potassium 730.5 mg; Sodium 292.1 mg.

The nutritional breakdown of this recipe falls within the criteria for the Heart Smart Restaurant Program.

Cowboy breakfast at the Hills Ranch, Cariboo.

Chicken Fajitas

Recommended BC Wine: Gray Monk – Gewurztraminer or
Mission Hill – Johannesberg Riesling.

1 tsp.	vegetable oil	5 mL
3 cups	diced, skinned and boned chicken breast	750 mL
2 cups	julienne strips of onions and green peppers	500 mL
1 tsp.	cajun spices	5 mL
1 tsp.	white wine	5 mL
1 tsp.	water	5 mL
2 cups	diced tomatoes	500 mL
8	warm flour tortillas	8
½ cup	sour cream	125 mL
¾ cup	homemade salsa	175 mL

Heat a pan with vegetable oil. Sauté chicken, onions, and green peppers. Add cajun spices – glaze with white wine and water – add diced tomatoes.

Fill warm tortillas with chicken mixture; roll up. Serve garnished with sour cream and salsa.

Per Serving: Protein 42.6 g; Fat 7.3 g; Carbohydrate 44.4 g; Kilocalories 430.8; Kilojoules 1802.5; Potassium 131.6 mg; Sodium 487.5 mg.

The nutritional breakdown of this recipe falls within the criteria for the Heart Smart Restaurant Program.

Fruits and berries of the Okanagan.

The boys of summer.

Restaurant at Peachland.

Honey Lemon Turkey Kabobs

½ lb.	smoked turkey breast	250 g
	sliced ¼-inch (0.5 cm) thick	
1	cantaloupe, cubed	1
24	seedless green grapes	24
¼ cup	vegetable oil	50 mL
2 tbsp.	lemon juice	30 mL
½ tsp.	ground ginger	2 mL
2 tsp.	honey	10 mL
	crisp lettuce	

Cut turkey into 1-inch (2.5 cm) squares. Thread turkey, cantaloupe and grapes alternately onto 8 wooden skewers. Combine oil, lemon juice, ginger and honey. Brush over turkey and fruit. Broil 5 minutes about 4 inches (10 cm) from heat, turning and brushing once. Arrange kabobs on lettuce and top with remaining dressing.   4 SERVINGS.

Heart Smart

Per Serving: Kilocalories 401.78; Fat 15.87 g; Sodium 836.85 mg; Protein 19.99 g; Carbohydrate 48.68 g; Potassium 871.19 mg.

Analysis done with 1/2 cup (125 mL) brown rice and 1 cup (250 mL) steamed broccoli.

The nutritional breakdown of this recipe falls within the criteria for the Heart Smart Restaurant Program.

Peachland Cheesecake Supreme

1	pkg. cream cheese	
	(250 g), softened	1
2	eggs	2
⅓ cup	sugar	75 mL
½ tsp.	almond flavoring	2 mL
½ cup	sour cream	125 mL
1 tbsp.	sugar	15 mL
¼ tsp.	almond flavoring	1 mL
4	fresh peaches, pitted and sliced	4

Beat together cream cheese, eggs, ⅓ cup (75 mL) sugar and ½ tsp. (2 mL) almond flavoring until smooth. Pour into 8 individual baking dishes, filling ⅔ full. Bake at 325°F (160°C) for 20 minutes. Remove from oven. Mix sour cream, 1 tbsp. (15 mL) sugar and ¼ tsp. (1 mL) almond flavouring. Spread over top of cheesecakes. Return to oven; bake 10 minutes longer. Chill before serving. To serve, arrange peach slices on cheesecakes.   8 SERVINGS.

Peachland peach cheesecake.

Haying at Armstrong.

Whole Wheat Cheddar Biscuits

2½ cups	whole wheat flour	625 mL
2 tsp.	baking powder	10 mL
½ tsp.	salt	2 mL
¼ cup	shortening	50 mL
½ cup	grated cheddar cheese	125 mL
1 cup	milk	250 mL
	sesame seeds	

In a large bowl, stir together flour, baking powder, and salt. Cut in shortening with a pastry blender until mixture resembles coarse crumbs. Stir in cheese until mixed throughout. Add milk all at once, stirring to make a soft dough. Turn dough onto a lightly floured board. Knead 8 - 10 times until smooth. Pat dough out to a ½-inch (1 cm) thickness. Cut out biscuits with a floured 2-inch (5 cm) cookie cutter. Place on a lightly greased baking sheet. Sprinkle with sesame seeds. Press lightly onto tops of biscuits. Bake at 425°F (220°C) for 15 - 18 minutes until lightly browned. MAKES 12 TO 15 BISCUITS.

Canoeing on Green Lake.

Mountains & Plateaus

British Columbia's mountains protect the Province's plateaus and alluvial valleys, dictate its weather and dominate its topography. In the east, from the 49th parallel to the Yukon border, rises the formidable beauty of the Rocky Mountains. Far to the west, the jagged, snowcapped Coast Mountains define British Columbia's Pacific coast. Between the two major ranges, chain after chain of rugged peaks rise from the plateau and valley. Offshore, the mountains of Vancouver Island and the Queen Charlotte Islands form the islands' spine.

Those who first ventured into the mountain regions relied on hunting and gathering to feed themselves. The strong, gamey taste of mountain sheep and goat, the firm freshwater trout and the juicy wild summer berries sustained early travellers. But winter wiped the landscape clean and few settlers chose to live deep in the mountains.

Although these lands yield to the plough with great reluctance, within the mountains lie pockets of fertile ground. Atlin, one of British Columbia's northernmost villages is a group of tidy, pastel-painted cottages huddled in the lee of the Coast Mountains. Gold first brought settlers to this remote pocket, and some stayed after the gold excitement waned. Today, around the rocky edges of Atlin's warm springs, watercress grows. In the warmed earth nearby, enterprising residents have planted gardens that are a glorious mixture of wild roses and beetroot, cabbages and columbine, potatoes and nasturtiums. Along the lakeshore, wild berries and chives grow.

Going out for a shoot, Vernon, at the turn of the century.

BCARS No. 63011.

Across the Province to the east, are the Kootenays, ridged by the Rocky, Purcell, Selkirk and Monashee mountains. While geologists explain that these chains emerged during a billion years of eruption and erosion, folklore is more fun. One tale suggests that Paul Bunyan left his gargantuan imprint on the Kootenays. He dug the Kootenay and Columbia rivers and Windermere lakes. With the dirt removed, he built the Rocky Mountains. He and his crew camped at Canal Flats where they used half a block as a stove

"The Seven Sisters" from Snake Road, Smithers.

to cook breakfast. The cooks strapped slabs of bacon on their feet to grease the griddle, and used steam shovels to ladle pancake batter out of concrete mixers.

Returning to the facts, we do know that the discovery of gold at Wild Horse Creek brought a flood of Europeans to the area. Prospectors rushed in, pursued by those who would feed or fleece them. Like miners everywhere, they gave higher priority to the search for riches than to preparing food. The typical mine cookhouse menu featured meat, vegetables, dried fruit, and lots of pastry. But as towns sprouted up around the prospector's camps, some establishments offered a little more elegance. The Windsor Hotel at Trout Lake City was run for 50 years by Alice Elizabeth Jowett, a widow who came from England in 1889. Mrs. Jowett's dining room gleamed with silverware and white tablecloths. Her roast beef and Yorkshire pudding were legendary. She, too, caught the gold fever and sometimes breadmaking was abandoned when she sallied forth to check her claims.

Today the Kootenays remain more conducive to hunting and fishing than to farming. Kootenay Lake, 145 kilometres long and shoehorned between the Selkirk and Purcell ranges, offers the largest rainbow trout in the world, the Gerrard Giants. Kokanee, whitefish, ling cod and Dolly Varden are also on the angler's menu.

The mountains are the barriers and backdrops to the plateaus. East of the Coast Mountains, west of the scrambled chains of the Cariboo, Purcell and Monashee mountains and north of the Cascades, the wide stretches of the Interior Plateau level out. This area between the mountain chains receives little more than 30 centimetres of precipitation a year. Without irrigation, agriculture is impossible, but the bunchgrass that shares the hills with sagebrush and pine is ideal for cattle.

At the plateau's southern end is the Nicola Valley. Before the arrival of Europeans, the Salish people fed on salmon returning to their spawning grounds. They also hunted deer and elk, eating some meat fresh and drying much for use. The thousands of lakes and streams that dot the plateau yielded trout. The Shuswap people held berry-picking dances to ensure the survival of the Saskatoon, chokecherry and hawthorn bushes.

The discovery of gold in the Cariboo in 1859 drew a horde of prospectors. In the gold rush's first years, miners and mules had to pack in anything that couldn't be provided by the land. Costs were high: flour at 30 cents and butter at a dollar a pound, a glass of whiskey for a dollar and a bottle of champagne for $60. Meanwhile, a good day's wages were $4.

Those who followed the prospectors up the Fraser and through the hills saw the potential of this vast, grassy plateau. Entrepreneurs established roadhouses along the miners' route. They also planted hay meadows, gardens and tiny orchards above the Thompson and Fraser rivers. These were irrigated by intricate systems that raised water from the river to the fields. Ranches soon spread out from the roadhouses as the newcomers discovered that the bunchgrass hills were ideal for cattle. By the late 1870's, ranchers were herding cattle over much of the plateau.

As ranchers took up the best land along the goldfields' route, others moved west, across the Fraser, into the Chilcotin. The Chilcotin was dream country. Settlers from faraway places were attracted to its promise of independence and solitude. Those who kept in mind the agricultural limitations of the plateau country prospered. Many, though, had dreams that couldn't be fulfilled. The challenges of a remote frontier overwhelmed them.

For more than 50 years, cattle drives were an annual Cariboo-Chilcotin feature. Livestock was herded to the railhead town of Ashcroft, finishing their journey to the coast in boxcars. The cattle industry still dominates the plateau, with white-faced Herefords poking their noses through rail fences from Ashcroft to Merritt to Quesnel to Riske Creek. Some of the world's largest ranches are found in the Cariboo-Chilcotin.

This background has led to a tradition of the working man's meal in the plateau country, though modern cooks work with more ingredients and flair than those of old. Pioneer cowboy Harry Marriott writes about his standard supper of rice, beans, fried pork and doughdodger bread, "with a little saucerful of prunes to top off the meal". One range cook was puzzled when his cowboys reported considerable intestinal distress after breakfast. But when he greased his pancake skillet with bacon grease instead of harness oil, the problem was solved.

Ranch and resort guests rest easier today. Barbecues featuring huge roasts, berry pies, tender steaks, homemade bread and gallons of coffee are featured at every guest ranch and rodeo. And some of the most sophisticated menus in British Columbia can be found at the ranches and wilderness retreats in the Province's mountains and plateaus.

BCARS No. 9525. *Harper's Grist Mill on the Thompson River.*

The Fraser at Lytton.

Penne with Beef Strips

¾ cup	penne or rigatoni pasta	175 mL
¼ lb.	sirloin steak, cut into thin strips	125 g
1 tsp.	vegetable oil	5 mL
1	garlic clove, minced	1
1 tbsp.	finely chopped onion	15 mL
¼	green pepper, cut into thin strips	¼
½ tsp.	dried basil	2 mL
½ tsp.	oregano or thyme	2 mL
1	medium tomato, chopped	1
	freshly ground pepper	
	freshly ground Parmesan cheese	

In a large pot of unsalted boiling water, cook pasta about 10 minutes. Meanwhile, in a small skillet, stir-fry beef in hot oil, over high heat for 1 to 2 minutes. Add garlic, onion, green pepper, basil and oregano or thyme. Cook 2 minutes longer or until beef is no longer pink. Add tomato and cook 1 to 2 minutes or until hot.

Drain pasta and toss with beef mixture. Season to taste with pepper and garnish with cheese. MAKES 1 SERVING.

Serve with raw veggie sticks.

Per Serving: Energy 385 Calories; Kilojoules 1610; Fat 12 g; Protein 35 g; Sodium 184 mg; Carbohydrate 34 g.

The nutritional breakdown of this recipe falls within the criteria for the Heart Smart Restaurant Program.

Cattle drive at Dead Man's Creek Valley.

Sourdough bread at Williams Lake.

Likely Sourdough Starter

3½ cups	all purpose flour	875 mL
1 tbsp.	sugar	15 mL
1	pkg. active dry yeast	1
2 cups	warm water	500 mL

In a large bowl, combine flour, sugar, and yeast. Gradually stir in warm water and beat until smooth. Cover bowl with plastic wrap. Let stand in a warm place for at least 3 days before using. To use, measure amount called for in recipe and follow recipe directions.

To replenish starter:

Add 1½ cups (375 mL) all purpose flour and 1 cup (250 mL) warm water to starter remaining in bowl. Beat until smooth. Cover with plastic wrap and let stand in a warm place. If starter is not used once a week, remove 1½ cups (375 mL) starter and follow steps for replenishing.

Sourdough Biscuits

1 cup	all purpose flour	250 mL
1 tbsp.	baking powder	15 mL
½ tsp.	baking soda	2 mL
½ tsp.	salt	2 mL
½ tsp.	sugar	2 mL
¼ cup	shortening	50 mL
1 cup	sourdough starter	250 mL
	melted butter	

In a large bowl, combine flour, baking powder, baking soda, salt, and sugar. Cut in shortening with a pastry blender until mixture resembles coarse crumbs. Stir in sourdough starter and mix to form a soft dough. Turn dough out onto a lightly floured board. Knead 8 to 10 times until smooth. Pat dough out to a ½-inch (1 cm) thickness. Cut out biscuits with a floured 2-inch (5 cm) cookie cutter. Place on a lightly greased baking sheet. Bake at 425°F (220°C) for 12 to 15 minutes until lightly browned.

Riske Creek Ranch Burgers

1 lb.	ground beef	500 g
1	egg	1
½ cup	fine dry bread crumbs	125 mL
¼ tsp.	salt	1 mL
	dash pepper	
¼ tsp.	chili powder	1 mL
4	hamburger buns, split	4
4	lettuce leaves	4
1	large tomato, finely chopped	1
1	jalapeño pepper, finely chopped	1
1 tbsp.	chopped onion	15 mL
1 tbsp.	chili sauce	15 mL

In a large bowl, mix ground beef, egg, bread crumbs, salt, pepper, and chili powder until well-combined. Form into 4 patties. Broil to desired doneness. Toast hamburger buns. For each serving, place lettuce leaves on bottoms of bun, top with a cooked burger. Mix tomato, jalapeño pepper, onion, and chili sauce. Spoon over burger and cover with top of bun. 4 SERVINGS.

Per Serving: Protein 36.5 g; Fat 19.6 g; Carbohydrate 41 g; Kilocalories 496; Potassium 538 mg; Sodium 656 mg.

The nutritional breakdown of this recipe falls within the criteria for the Heart Smart Restaurant Program when lean ground beef is used.

Haying near Armstrong.

Mountains at Ashcroft.

Pan-fried trout at upper Arrow Lakes.

Slocan Grilled Trout

¼ cup	butter, divided	50 mL
3	green onions, chopped	3
2 cups	sliced mushrooms	500 mL
2 tbsp.	lemon juice	30 mL
1 tbsp.	minced parsley	15 mL
4	trout, about 6 oz./ 180 g each	4

Melt half the butter in a small skillet at medium-low heat. Add green onions and mushrooms. Sauté until tender. Add lemon juice and parsley. Keep warm over low heat. Rinse trout, pat dry and dredge with flour. Heat remaining butter in a large skillet at medium heat. Fry trout about 6 to 7 minutes per side until flesh flakes easily. To serve, place trout on a serving dish and spoon mushroom mixture over top. 4 SERVINGS.

Houston, Bulkley Valley.

Bannock

2 cups	flour	500 mL
½ tsp.	salt	2 mL
2 tsp.	baking powder	10 mL
3 tbsp.	lard	45 mL
⅔ - ¾ cups	water	150 - 175 mL

Mix dry ingredients together. Work lard in as if making pie dough. Add water. Shape dough with floured hands into flat biscuits. Baked on greased baking sheet in a 400°F (200°C) oven for 20-25 minutes.

Slocan Apple Muffins

2 cups	flour	500 mL
1 tbsp.	baking powder	15 mL
¼ tsp.	salt	1 mL
½ cup	sugar	125 mL
¼ tsp.	cinnamon	1 mL
¼ tsp.	nutmeg	1 mL
1	egg, beaten	1
1 cup	milk	250 mL
⅓ cup	melted butter or cooking oil	75 mL
1 cup	peeled, chopped apple	250 mL

Sift together flour, baking powder, salt, sugar, cinnamon, and nutmeg. Combine egg, milk, and melted butter or cooking oil. Stir into dry ingredients just until moistened. Stir in apple. Spoon into lightly greased muffin tins, filling ¾ full. Bake at 400°F (200°C) for 15 to 20 minutes. MAKES 12 TO 15 MUFFINS.

Fly fishing at Dutch Creek at Fairmont Hot Springs.

Rudolph's Bakery in Nakusp.

Versatile Broccoli Soup

1 lb.	broccoli chopped	500 g
1 cup	beef bouillon	250 mL
⅔ cup	chopped onion	150 mL
⅓ cup	chopped celery	75 mL
⅓ cup	chopped green pepper	75 mL
1 tbsp.	butter or margarine	15 mL
2 cups	milk	500 mL
1 tsp.	salt or to taste	5 mL
1¼ cups	light cream	300 mL
	sour cream for topping, if desired	
	chopped chives for topping, if desired	

Cook broccoli in bouillon until tender – approximately 10 minutes. In small skillet, sauté onion, celery and green pepper in butter or margarine until onion is tender but not browned.

If serving soup hot: combine cooked broccoli with broth, onion mixture, milk, salt and cream in saucepan. Heat through gently, but do not boil. Serve either as is or garnish with spoonfuls of sour cream and chopped chives.

If serving soup cold, combine cooked broccoli with broth, onion mixture, milk, salt and cream in large bowl. Refrigerate until well-chilled. Serve either as is or garnished with swirls of sour cream and chopped chives.

MAKES 6 SERVINGS.

Mountain Potato Nuggets with Sun-Dried Tomato Vinaigrette

This new potato dish may be served hot as a side dish or chilled as a salad. When new potatoes are unavailable, try small red or white potatoes.

2 lbs.	small new potato nuggets	1 kg
1 tbsp.	balsamic vinegar	15 mL
1 tsp.	Dijon mustard	5 mL
1	garlic clove, minced	1
¼ cup	olive oil from bottled sun-dried tomatoes	50 mL
¼ cup	slivered, drained sun-dried tomatoes (packed in oil)	50 mL
¼ tsp.	each salt and pepper	1 mL
⅓ cup	fresh slivered basil	75 mL
½ cup	shredded Asiago cheese	125 mL

Scrub unpeeled potatoes. Boil 15 to 20 minutes or until tender; drain, reserving 1 tbsp. (15 mL) potato water.

Meanwhile, in small bowl, whisk together vinegar, mustard, garlic and reserved potato water. Whisk in oil, sun-dried tomatoes and salt and pepper.

In large bowl, toss warm potatoes, vinaigrette and ¼ cup (50 mL) of the basil. Taste and adjust seasoning. Transfer to platter or large serving bowl; top with cheese and remaining basil. May be served hot or chilled. MAKES 4 SERVINGS.

From the summit of the Roger's Pass Highway.

Cattle at Cedarvale.

Hay bales Prince George.

Veal with Lemon Sauce

1 tbsp.	cooking oil	15 mL
1	medium onion, sliced	1
4	veal chops, cut ½-inch (1 cm) thick	4
1	chicken bouillon cube, crushed	1
1 tbsp.	lemon juice	15 mL
	dash salt and pepper	
½ cup	boiling water	125 mL
1 tbsp.	flour	15 mL
2	egg yolks	2

Heat half the oil in a large skillet at medium heat. Add onion; sauté until tender. Set aside. Add remaining oil to skillet. Brown veal chops on both sides. Add onion, bouillon cube, lemon juice, salt, pepper and water in skillet. Reduce heat and simmer, covered, 40 minutes until veal is tender. Remove veal; keep warm. Pour pan juices into a small bowl; skim off fat, reserving 1 tbsp. (15 mL). Return measured fat to skillet. Blend in flour. Gradually add pan juices and stir until slightly thickened. In a small bowl, whip egg yolks until well blended. Whip a small amount of hot sauce into egg yolks, then beat egg yolks into hot sauce in skillet. Cook and stir until thick but do not boil. To serve, place veal on a warm serving dish and spoon sauce over. MAKES 4 SERVINGS.

Heart Smart

Per Serving: Protein 21.5 g; Fat 18.8 g; Carbohydrate 3.5 g; Kilocalories 273.5; Potassium 410 mg; Sodium 264 mg.

The nutritional breakdown of this recipe falls within the criteria for the Heart Smart Restaurant Program.

Kispiox Valley Near Hazelton.

The Crying Woman's Totem Pole at Kitspiox.

Roadhouse Burgundy Beef

1	beef cross-rib roast,	1
	3 lb./1.5 kg	
3 tbsp.	cooking oil	45 mL
½ cup	burgundy	125 mL
3 tbsp.	chili sauce	45 mL
¼ cup	finely chopped onion	50 mL
1	clove garlic, minced	1
½ tsp.	salt	2 mL
¼ tsp.	pepper	1 mL

Pierce meat with a fork. Place in a large deep bowl. Combine remaining ingredients and pour over beef. Cover and marinate overnight, turning meat occasionally. Place beef in a roasting pan; pour marinade over. Roast, covered, at 325°F (160°C) for about 1½ hours until beef is tender and reaches an internal temperature of 150°F (65°C). 8 SERVINGS.

The Bauern House Restaurant in Kimberley.

Scow Bread

8 cups	flour	2000 mL
½ cup	baking powder	125 mL
2 tsp.	salt	10 mL
1 cup	margarine	250 mL
7 cups	water	1750 mL
1	can (385 mL) evaporated milk	1

Mix water and milk together and add it to the flour and other ingredients. Dough should be wet. Pat down (do not overwork) and cut into desired shapes. Bake at 350°F (180°C) for 20 minutes. MAKES APPROXIMATELY 40 PIECES.

A wheat field.

Near Lillooet.

Ashcroft Potatoes

6	large baking potatoes	6
1 tbsp.	cooking oil	15 mL
1	small onion, chopped	1
1	green pepper, chopped	1
1 cup	sliced mushrooms	250 mL
1	medium tomato, chopped	1
	salt and pepper to taste	
	minced parsley	

Clean potatoes and bake in a 350°F (180°C) oven for about 1 hour until tender. When potatoes are nearly ready, heat oil in a medium skillet at medium heat. Add the onion, green pepper and mushrooms. Stir-fry about 7 minutes until tender. Add tomato; cook 3 minutes longer. To serve, split each potato down centre and spoon hot vegetable mixture on top. Add salt and pepper to taste. Sprinkle parsley over.

6 SERVINGS.

Char-Grilled Quail

Recommended BC Wine: Calona Wines – Rougeon '88, Gray Monk – Chardonnay or Domaine de Chaberton – Pinot Blanc.

Zesty Italian Salad Dressing
quail (2 per person as a guideline)

Split quail up the backbone. Dip in salad dressing, place on hot grill and cook for approximately 5 minutes, turn and baste with dressing. Cook until done. Every grill is different, so experiment with cooking time.

Roasted Quail

quail (two per person as a guideline)
soy sauce
freshly grated ginger root
minced garlic cloves

Mix together soy sauce, ginger and garlic and pour over the quail in an oven-proof baking dish. Bake in oven at 350°F (180°C) for 30 minutes. Baste several times during cooking.

Kokanee spawning in the Kootenay River.

Gang Ranch.

Burns Lake Ground Beef Salad

1 lb.	ground beef	500 g
½ cup	chopped onion	125 mL
2 tbsp	chopped green chili pepper	30 mL
1	can (14 oz./398 mL) stewed tomatoes	1
¾ tsp	chili powder	3 mL
1 tsp.	oregano	5 mL
1	can (5½ oz./156 mL) tomato paste tortilla chips	1
1	small head lettuce, shredded grated cheddar cheese	1

In a large skillet at medium heat, brown ground beef until it loses its pink color. Add onion and chili pepper. Cook and stir for 5 minutes. Drain excess fat. Add stewed tomatoes with juice to the skillet, breaking in small pieces with a fork. Add chili powder, oregano, and tomato paste, stirring to mix well. Reduce heat and simmer 15 minutes. To serve, layer tortilla chips, lettuce, and meat mixture in large bowls. Garnish with grated cheese. 6 SERVINGS.

Gang Ranch near Williams Lake.

"The Black Tusk" at Garibaldi Park.

Mushroom Asparagus Crêpes

...the taste of Spring with a touch of elegance.

Crêpes:

2	eggs	2
½ cup	no-additive/all-purpose flour	125 mL
2 tbsp.	oat bran	25 mL
¼ tsp.	basil	1 mL
1 cup	milk	250 mL

Filling:

½ cup	thinly sliced celery	125 mL
1 cup	sliced mushrooms	250 mL
¼ cup	chopped onion	50 mL
2 tbsp.	margarine	25 mL
2 tbsp.	no-additive/all-purpose flour	25 mL
¼ tsp.	salt	1 mL
⅛ tsp.	pepper	.5 mL
1½ cups	milk	375 mL
½ cup	grated Cheddar cheese	125 mL
36	asparagus spears	36

Garnish:

2	hard-cooked eggs, sliced	2

Crêpes: Beat eggs slightly, add no-additive/all-purpose flour, oat bran and basil. Gradually stir in milk; let mixture stand for a minimum of 15 minutes.

Pour about ¼ cup (50 mL) batter onto hot skillet and quickly rotate pan to spread batter evenly over bottom. Cook until top is dry and underside golden. Turn crêpe and cook for a few seconds on the other side. Continue cooking remaining batter in same fashion.

Filling: Sauté celery, mushrooms and onion in margarine until just tender. Stir in no-additive/all-purpose flour, salt and pepper. Gradually add milk, stirring constantly until thickened. Add cheese and continue to stir until cheese has melted.

Cook asparagus until just tender in boiling water. Drain. Be sure sauce and asparagus are hot, then on each crêpe, arrange 3 asparagus spears and about 2 tbsp. (25 mL) sauce. Roll up crêpe and arrange 3 crêpes on each plate. Spoon sauce over crêpes and garnish with egg slices. Serve hot.
YIELD: 4 SERVINGS OF 3 CRÊPES/SERVING.

The mouth of the Columbia River in the Rocky Mountains.

The many fine British Columbia food products used in this book
are represented by the following Boards and Commissions:
- BC Chicken Marketing Board
- BC Cranberry Marketing Board
- BC Egg marketing Board
- BC Grape Marketing Board
- BC Hog Commission
- BC Milk Marketing Board (Milk and Dairy Products)
- BC Mushroom Marketing Board
- BC Oyster Board
- BC Sheep and Wool Commission
- BC Tree Fruit Marketing Board
- BC Turkey Marketing Board
- BC Vegetable Marketing Commission

Other segments of BC agriculture, fisheries & food:
- BC Cattlemans Association
- BC Salmon Marketing Council
  plus Shellfish, Trout and Sole
- Ginseng Growers
- Quail Producers
- Raspberry Growers
- Blueberry Council
- Western Greenhouse Growers
- BC Wine Institute
- Rogers Natural Foods – Grains
- Apiculture (Honey)
- Heart and Stroke Foundation
- BC Shellfish Growers Association
- British Columbia Salmon Farmers Association
- Commercial Fishing Industry Council
- Fisheries Council of BC
- Pacific Seafood Council
- United Fisherman and Allied Workers Union
- Pacific Trollers Association
- BC Fruit Growers' Association
- BC Pork Producers' Association
- BC Nursery Trades Association